# Armageddon

by

W.B. Godbey

*First Fruits Press*
*Wilmore,*
*Kentucky*
*c2017*

*Armageddon.*
By W.B. Godbey.
First Fruits Press, © 2017
Digital version at http://place.asburyseminary.edu/godbey/4/

ISBN: 9781621717225 (print), 9781621717232 (digital), 9781621717249 (kindle)

For all other uses, contact:

First Fruits Press
B.L. Fisher Library
Asbury Theological Seminary
204 N. Lexington Ave.
Wilmore, KY 40390
http://place.asburyseminary.edu/firstfruits

**Godbey, W. B. (William Baxter), 1833-1920.**
Armageddon / by W.B. Godbey. – Wilmore, KY : First Fruits Press, ©2017.
37 pages ; cm.
Armageddon -- Rapture of the saints -- War of the kings -- Fall of Satan and all the kings.
Reprint. Previously published: Greensboro, North Carolina. : Apostolic Messenger Office, [190-?].
ISBN: 9781621717225 (pbk.)
1. End of the world. 2. Rapture (Christian eschatology)  I. Title.
BT875.G62 2017                                                                          220.1

Cover design by Jon Ramsey

asburyseminary.edu
800.2ASBURY
204 North Lexington Avenue
Wilmore, Kentucky 40390

*First Fruits*
THE ACADEMIC OPEN PRESS OF ASBURY SEMINARY

First Fruits Press
*The Academic Open Press of Asbury Theological Seminary*
204 N. Lexington Ave., Wilmore, KY 40390
859-858-2236
first.fruits@asburyseminary.edu
asbury.to/firstfruits

# ARMAGEDDON

By

## W. B. Godbey

*AUTHOR OF*
*'New Testament Commentaries'' ''New Testament*
*Translation,'' and a great number of*
*other books and booklets.*

Published by
THE APOSTOLIC MESSENGER OFFICE
900 SILVER RUN AVE.
Greensboro, North Carolina

# ARMAGEDDON

Acts II Ch. tell us, that when Jesus had wrought His mighty works on bloody Calvary, gone down to hell and proclaimed His victory to Satan and all his myrmidons and thus triumphed over the powers of darkness verifying Phil. 2:10 "Every knee shall bow and every tongue confess of things in heaven, in earth and beneath the earth;" having thus proclaimed His victory in the Pandemonium and fulfilled His promise to the saved thief dying by His side, "This day thou shalt be with me in paradise;" having thus proclaimed His victory in the regions of woe, crossing the chasm Luke 16:24 which Abraham told Dives no finite being could cross and thus escape out of hell; He entered the intermediate paradise, where He met all the patriarchs and prophets except Enoch and Elisha who had been honored with a translation gone up to heaven with their bodies.

(a) Having enjoyed an infinitely glorious Sabbath with them the ensuing midnight, he abolishes that intermediate paradise, denominated Abraham's Bosom; became Himself as to be the "first fruits of them that slept;" therefore the O. T. saints could not go up to heaven until he had finished the work of redemption; fulfilling the Abrahamic covenant; therefore they went into that intermediate paradise in upper Hades, Abraham's Bosom, Lower Hades, Tophet, the bottomless pit.

(b) Eph IV:8,10 "He that ascended is the same also who first descended into the lower parts of the earth; leading captivity captive and giving gifts unto the people." Thus we see His descension began way down in lower Hades, ascending into upper Hades and there giving them a glorious Sabbath day and night; unutterably delectable as they had all spent their whole lives looking for

Him and died without the sight. Thus at midnight He began His wonderful ascension; stopping at Jerusalem and receiving His body on the resurrection morn; then tarrying 40 days, during which we hear very little of Him as He was never with His disciples but a few times; never having spent a night with them; the solution is patent; He had a heap of company, all those O. T. saints, in a 40 days camp meeting; Himsef only visible, as they were invisible, disembodied and will so remain till the first resurrection, for which we are on the constant outook.

(c) When He ascended up from Mt. Olivet they all accompanied Him in His triumphant flight; the prophetic eye of David being permitted Ps. ch. 24 to behold the glorious scene and hear them shout as they approach the celestial metropolis, "Lift up your heads Oh ye gates and be ye lifted up ye everlasting doors and let the king of glory come in!" The angel porters promptly respond, "Who is this King of Glory? To which the host answers back: "He is the Lord Mighty to save and strong to deliver;" then the gates are lifted high and swing wide, when the conqueror of Mt. Calvary enters with a triumphant tread, Abraham on his right and Job on his left and the long procession of O. T. saints following with tremendous shouts of victory; reciprocated by millions of unfallen angels, from myriads of worlds that never knew sin nor sorrow, having come thither to witness the grandest ovation, heavenly hierarchies ever knew, i. e. the royal triumph of king Jesus victorious from the bloody altitudes of Calvary. Amid this tremendous ovation, He leads up the sacramental host, and halts before the great white throne, with the response, "Here am I father and the children Thou hast given me!"

He responds, "Well done my son, thou

didst create that world and Satan invaded and captured it. As thou hast redeemed us with thy blood, it is thine forever; sit thou on my right hand, till I make thine enemies thy footstool.

"d" He is sitting there this day; but the culminating prophecies unanimously enforce the conclusion of the imminent fulfillment of that promise Dan. 7:9, "I beheld til the thrones were cast down and the Ancient of Days did sit; a fiery stream went before Him, and a thousand thousand ministred unto Him." The Holy Spirit has five symbols, wind, water, fire, oil, and wine, of which the fire means sanctification; because it is the great destroyer and in sanctification sin is destroyed, burnt up utterly exterminated. In this passage it symbolizes the awful destruction that will come when the whole world in the last days of the Gentile dispensation; eliminating out of it all the in corrigibes and unsavables, as we have seen in the winding up of all preceding dispensations; the antediluvian, by the flood, taking away the people who had resisted the preaching of Nor or Noah 120 years; thus proving their own incorrigibility; the postdiluvian patriarchy, in the awful plagues of Egypt rolling in 10 successive epochs, death and destruction, eliminating out of the world the people who would not heed the preaching of Moses, Aaron, and Miriam the prophetic family nor the brilliant examples of Abraham, Isaac, Jacob, Melchizedek, Jethro and Job; having proved; hopelessly wedded to their idols; their removal was a **sine qua non to** the ingress of the theocracy, under Moses.

(e) Likewise at the close of the Jewish dispensation, behold the awful tribulation which lasted 7 years; meanwhile at Jerusalem alone a round million perished by the sword, pestilence and famine, 90,000 sold into slavery, the scathed and peeled remnant, led captive to Rome to grace the triumph of Titus and become the crown slaves of the empire.

(f) The antediluvian was the skylight dispensation with no written; but God in person speaking to the person. The postdiluvian patriarchy, reached a higher plane, the **ipse dixit** of Jehovah to the patriarchs. In so many cases Abraham, Isaac, Jacob, Job, Melchizedek, thus pertinently illustrated by the bursting starlight, auxiliary to the beautiful azure sky of the former dispensation; followed by the glorious rising moon, climbing the skies and walking in her queenly majesty among the glittering constellations; thus superinducing the increasing divine right of the written law so copiously given by the great Jehovah, face to face with Moses on Mt. Sinai; his face retaining the unutterable divine radiance; when he descended from the Mt., so the people of Israel could not behold the glory of His countenance and He found it necessary to protect their failing eyes by a veil dropped over His face.

(g) The moonlit dispensation of Moses having cultured the people for a higher and brighter attitude in the unsearchable revelations of the Almighty; the day dawns with the brilliant and unprecedented ministry of John the Baptist, permitted to rise to a higher plane than His precesessors, soon followed by the star of Bethlehem, with its beautiful and wonderful effulgence proving the auspicious precursor of the glorious Son of Righteousness rising on the dark, superstitions and wicked world, with healing in His wings; John permitted to enjoy the glorious honor of His introduction to the world and inauguration into His official messiahship; thus permitting Him to anoint Him for the high priesthood on which He proceeded at once to enter; walking into the temple, with

the authority of the high priest to cast out  the
buyers and sellers and thus purify the house of the
Lord.  His wonderful ministry those memoroable
3 years, filling the earth with His fame, brought
the people in multitudes from the ends of the earth,
meanwhile he pours the light of day on the sight-
less eye ball, causes the deaf to hear, the dumb to
speak, the lame man to leap as an hart, the lepers
to be cleansed, the dead to rise and live again, and
the poor to have the gospel preached  unto them;
finally culminating in the glorious baptisms of the
Holy Ghost and fire, when 3,000 were converted in
the A. M. 5,000 in the P. M., and the  120  so
wonderfully filled with the Holy Ghost, that the unprecedented power with which they  spoke  was
brilliantly illustrated by forked tongues of fire sitting on their heads; Thus inaugurating  the glo-
riouos Gospel dispensation significantly denominated the kingdom of heaven, actually set up in human
hearts here on the earth; the Holy Ghost, having
in bygone ages operated on people  extrinsically,
i. e from without, and sometimes exceedingly po-
tently, actually picking up a prophet and carrying
him away and drop him on some lonely Mt. or
dry bone valley; but now with the glorious pente-
costal dispensation, He comes in and takes up His
abode in the human heart; thus verifying the still
small voice, that Eliah heard on Mt. Horeb when
he stood in the mouth of the cave and covered his
face with his mantle and God came to him  and
thus speaking told him to  go  back  to the land
of Israel and call Elisha to succeed him in  his
prophetic office,  anoint Jehu  to  be  king  over
Israel, and Haziel to be king of Syria.

(h) When this wonderful transition, out of the
law into the Gospel dispensation; from  the types
and shadows, symbols and ordinances, into the glorious dispensation of the Holy Ghost( when instead

of speaking to a prophet in an age, the enthroned interceding Savior sends him to every broken heart, contrite spirit, and humble believing soul, to enlighten, sanctify, empower and give victory; thus raising up armies of prophets; in order that this glorious transition, from bleeding birds and beasts, on Jewish altars slain 4,000 years to the bleeding Lamb of Calvary, who fulfilled all the antecedent types and shadows; 250,000 lambs as Josephus says sacrificed in a single passover, in the 1500 years of its dispensation, giving us the enormous number of 370 million innocent all bleeding and dying to typify the Lamb of Calvary, thus quantity so copiously substituted for quality; Solomon upon the dedication of the temple having slaughtered 120,000 sheep and 22,000 oxen Oh what a wonderful transition, out of symbolic legalism into glorious heartfelt experimental realizations; making the supernatural birth the glorious privilege of every contrite believing penitent and entire sanctification the transcendent victory of every humble pilgrim who will take it by faith and shout Satan out of countenance.

(h) Thus in order to reach this **high plane of** God's kingdom in the heart, the sweet simplicity of redeeming grace and redeeming love for every soul, without the encumbrance of the great burdensome ritual of Sinai and Moses; thus you see, in order to the grand transition into the glorious gospel Holy Ghost dispensation; the great Jewish tribulation, seven long years; blood constantly flowing in river and the people falling so rapidly by the sword, pestilences and famines, that they could not bury them. Consequently at Jerusalem the pestilential exhalations from the unburied corpses so poisoned the atmosphere, that the people fell dead in piles. In this way the high priests, proud Pharises, dictatorial scribes, who had rejected Jesus and fought him all his life, were cut down and taken out of the world. If they had lived they would have antagonized the disciples and thrown every possible inpedement in the way of the Gospel church. Therefore in order to the successful launching of the Gospel church, that awful destruction had to come. They were so utterly and completely dominated by Satan, that they actually believed he was God and gave him their adoration and obedience

(i) Such are the concurrent testimonies of the prophecies as to assure us that we are walking on the ragged edges of the Gentile dispensation, amid the glorious dawn of the millennium; the lunar chronology, which measures time by the revoloutions of the moon around the earth and is used by the patriarchs and prophets Christ and His apostles, already makes the rapture of the saints over due sixty-nine years; the calendar chronology measured by the revolution of the planets round the sun and used in Europe, making it ovoer due twenty-seven years, while the solar chonology measuring time by the revolutions of the earth arouond the sun and used in America, makes the rapture of the saints due in nineteen hundred and twenty-three only eight years hence.

(j) Daniel 12 ch. tells us "there be a time of trouble, such as the world never knew before and never will know again;" but that Michael the commander of the resurrection angels will stand up, and every one whose name is written in the book i. e. on the bride roll will be delivered, from that awful time of trouble. Thus admonished by the inspired prophets of the Most High we have every reason to be on the constant outlook for His glorious appearing, to take His waiting bride; as soon as this is done, the great tribulation will at once set in.

## Chapter I.

## RAPTURE OF THE SAINTS

Mat 24:29 "Immediately after the desolation of those days the sun will be darkened and the moon will not give her light and the stars will be falling."

In the prophecies the sun symbolizes the Kings, the moon, the queens and the stars the subordinate department of the governments this scripture is in our Lord's sermon which he preached on Mt. Olivet on Wednesday afternoon before His crucifixion and recorded by Mat. 24 and 25 chs. Mark 13 ch. and Luke 21 ch. The E. V. says tribulation. In my translation you will find it reads desolation. The Greek **thlipsis** has both these meanings.

The objection to rendering it tribulation, consists in the fact that the people would think it meant the great Gentile tribulation which has not yet come on the earth but which we are on the constant outlook whereas it refers to the Jewish tribulation which took place A. D. 66-73, running seven years during which they utterly desolated the whole country leaving it a heap of ruins, Jerusalem, the temple and all the cities; believing that the Jews would give it up and never try to get it back; as they sold them into slavery and carried into captivity all who survived, the sword, pestilence and famine, because they would revolt under those fake Christs who are constantly arising. Rome made it a rule to exterminate every nation which she could not rule and thus enforce her government on the whole world. When they had desolated the land and exterminated all the Jews out of it, as it was a penalty of death for a Jew to be found any where in Palestine or any other country traveling with his face toward Jerusalem, he was taken up and killed. Thus they utterly exterminated them all. Then the Bedouin Arabs, the children of Abraham through Ishmael Esau and his second wife Kitura poured in from Arabia, because the land of Canaan was so much richer and more fruitful and better in every respect and have been there every since.

(k) They never live in houses, but always in tents; because father Abraham never lived in a house, but spent his whole life in a tent, which he carried from place to place on a camels back, setting it up where God told him and staying there till he bid him go on whither He would lead him. The reason why Paul could make money enough by his trade, tent building to support him and Luke, Timothy and Silas his helpers was because the Bedouin Arabs are the largest nation in all the country this day; all living in tents everywhere, and believing that they would lose their souls, if they should depart from the faith and practice of father Abraham who never did live in a house. For that reason the cities destroyed by the Romans in the Jewish tribulation remained desolate till the Jews have very recently come back from their wanderings in every nation under heaven and rebuilt their old cities occupied by their ancestors in the good olden times. When I first went to that country twenty years ago, they were just beginning to come back and rebuild every thing. It is just wonderful how the old cites have leaped into life; as the Jews are the greatest builders in the world and build nothing but the best and most substantial houses; Jerusalem having been quadrupled in size in the last twenty years and the cities throughout all the land which were a heap of ruin have wonderfully leaped into life. This fact is exceedingly

ominous of the Lord's speedy coming as these
scriptures from the lips of our Savior certify that
immediately after the desolation of those days, The
sun will be darkened and the moon will not give
her light and the stars wil be falling, i. e. king
queens and potentates will totter and fall from their
thrones as Daniel 7:9 "I beheld till· the thrones
were cast down and the ancient of days did sit" i. e.
God will come down and shake the kings from
their thrones to vacate them for His Son. We
certainly do realize a wonderful shaking now. In
the great Orient where the teaming millions dwell
they are not only tottering but falling from their
thrones each revolving day; meanwhile there is an
ominous shaking throughout the new world,
and unsteadiness in all the governments of the
globe this day, a trembling and quaking evidently
superinduced by the unseen power that sets
us and takes down kings in all the earth. In this
chapter Matt. 24:29, 35 where He says immediately after the desolation of these days. The
snu will be darkened the moon will not give her
light, stars wil be falling i.e. kings, queens, satraps
and governors will be falling from their thrones;
the next verse says "Then will the sign of the
Son of man appear in the heavens." N. B. the sign
and Himself are different phenomena; the former
will be something after the order of the star of
Bethlehem seen by the wise men of the east; but
as His second coming will be so much more glorious
than His first, doubtless it will assume the manifes-
tation of a grand Aurora borealis such as never
before seen; attracting the attention of the as-
tronomical world and focalizing all the telescopes
to sweep through it and diagnose it to their ut-
most ability. This is the first phenomenon and will
doubtless simply be the splendor of his own person-
al glory, radiated out millions of miles before

Him; as we must bear in mind that when He comes for His bride, He does not come to the earth but only in calling distance as you see in 1. Thess. 4: "Then will the Lord Himself descend from Heaven with a shout, with the trumpet of God and the voice of the Arch Angel, and the dead in Christ will rise first. Then we who are alive and left on the earth will be caught to meet the Lord in the air and thus be forever with the Lord. These things exhort ye one another." Here we see that the Lord doesn't come to earth but we are caught up to meet Him. The word **kelensnia** translated shout is very strong and means the shout of an army general to his soldiers and also the shout of a sea captain to his sailors and a hunter to his dogs. In all those cases the man shouts to the very top of his voice and of course he could shout loud enough for us to hear him a million miles away. And the splendor of His glorified person will be manifested at a vast distance through ethereal space. The next verse says, "Then will all the nations and tribes of the earth weep and wail, when they see the Son of man coming in the clouds with power and great glory." By this time He has advanced near enough for us to recognize His person whereas hitherto we only saw the light radiating from it. This corroborates Rev. 1:7, "Every eye shall behold Him." As He shall be out in the firmament, the earth revolving will enable all the people in the world in 24 hours. Then the next verse says "He will send forth His angels and they will scour the whole earth from the rising of the sun to the going down of the same from the extremities of the heavens unto the extremities of the same and gather up His elect." This verse plainly and unequivocally reveals the rapture of the saints, gathered by the resurrection angels from every land and clime; from Abel (whose tomb

I have repeatedly seen) and father Noe (whose tomb I have seen); gathering the holy family Abraham and Sarah, Isaac and Rebekah, Jacob and Leah from the cave of Mt. Pelah and great Mt. Olivet the largest in all the land of Canaan the burial ground of Israel from ages immemorial; whose patriarchs and prophets are awaiting the trumpet call will all leap into life with tremendous shouts of victory.

(e) Throughout the Bible Gabriel always appears in the interest of humanity and Michael in co-operation with divine government. Jude 9 tells us that when God wanted Moses to stand with his son and Elijah on the Mt. of transfiguration to represent all the people who will be transfigured through the resurrection; Elijah by his side representing all who will be transfigured through the translation; Daniel 12; 1, 3 describing this great tribulation, assures us that every one whose name is written in the book i. e. on the bride roll will be delivered; at the same time recognizing Michael standing up commanding the resurrection angels in their flight to the ends of the earth ransacking mountain, plain, deserts, oceans, seas, and gathering all the saints resting in the dust of every land in their pinions of light and escorting them away to meet the Lord in the air; meanwhile the living pilgrims in every land are gazing upon the scene, with unutterable bewilderment, as the resurrected saints will all be visible and exceedingly conspicuous, as we see abundantly revealed in the transfiguration, when Peter, James and John were permitted to behold His glory, Moses and Elijah in similar investiture, standing by His side; meanwhile their brilliancy actually eclipsed the mortal vision of the Apostles, so they fell on their faces and hid their eyes from the transcendent effulgence. The scene will be utterly glorious, lighting the whole world as if a 1,000 suns had turned in from worlds of darkness.

(m) I Cor. 15:51 "We shall not all sleep, but we shall all be changed in a moment, in the twinkling of an eye, this mortal shall put on immortality, this corruption shall put on incoorruption and mortality shall be swallowed up of life." Here we see the translation of the living saints wrought by the omnipotent Holy Spirit will be instantaneous, i. e. in the twinkling of an eye. We will thus suddenly undergo this wonderful metamorphism, like the caterpillar, turning to a butterfly, spreading its wings and flying away; bidding eternal adieu to its former living on green leaves and cess pools, to wing its flight amid the blooming flowers and live on honey, 104 lbs. Avoirdupois hold this body in which I dwell on **terra firma.** When my translation comes, in a happy surprise I'll find myself flying through the air, as I have often dreamed, even from my childhood, during the ambrosial slumbers of the fleeting night, thinking that I was flying like a bird through the air, over hills, valleys, tree tops, barking dogs, bleating flocks and lowing herds, till I would light somewhere on a mountain slope.

(n) We should all live in constant anticipation of the sounding trumpet, calling us to rise and fly and meet the Lord in the air. In the present life, our caterpillar state, this body is the tenement of the **psychee** (soul, consisting of the physical life, the intellect, the memory, the judgment and the figured will be the tenement of the **pneuma,** (our immortal spirit) i. e. the man himself, consisting of the conscience, the will and the affections and of course still identified with the **psychee** with all of its wonderful intelectual and educational enduements end acquisitions, itself also spiritualized, so that we will never have any weight any more nor be obstructed by material impediments; but wing our flight like angels from world to world on missions of love and mercy, responsively to the **ipse dixit** of our blessed heavenly Father. Reader are you ready to hear the trumpet blow and see the Lord coming in a cloud or would you as He says Matt. 24 ch. in His valedictory sermon on His second coming, be a member of the nations and tribes who will weep and wail when they see Him coming? If you will read that ch., you will find the very next verse says "He will send His angels and they will gather His elect from the four winds of the earth, from the extremities of the heavens unto the extremities of the same." 1 Pet. ch. 1 says "We are elect through the sanctification of the spirit, in harmony with Matt. 25; 1, 13 who tells that the wise virgins will go up to meet the Lord in the air, and the foolish i. e. those who thought one work of grace was enough and failed to have their vessels filled with oil i. e. their hearts filled with the Holy Ghost. Therefore while the nations girdling the world will be weeping and wailing and calling for the rocks and mts. to afll on them and hide them from the face of Him sitting on the cloud; the wholy sanctified will be caught to meet the Lord in the air and as Paul says 1 Thess. 4: be forever with the Lord.

---

## Chapter II.

## WAR OF THE KINGS.

When the rapture of the saints shall have transpired, the kings will all quickly fall from their thrones, Dan 7;9, "I behold, till the thrones were cast down and the Ancient of Days did sit; a fiery stream went before Him and a thousand thousand ministered unto Him." Here you see the fulfillment of God's promise to His son, when He ascended up from Mt. Olivet and reported His work Acts ch. 2; the Father responding, "Thou hast done all things well; conquered Satan, and saved that lost world, so it is thine alone forever; therefore sit Thou on my right hand till I make thine enemies thy footstool." His enemies are all His disloyal subjects and especially including the incumbents of all the thrones on the earth, ruling them as Satan's subordinates. Consequently when Father verifies this promise, He will shake down every potentate in all the earth; co-operated by these million destroying angels, in the execution of His righteous judgments viz. the wicked nations and fallen churches. We certainly have this day in the world wide discontentment, gendering revolution and the great Oriental Wars, ominous adumbrations of these terrific prophetical fulfillments, destined to transpire in the latter days of the Gentile dispensation; on whose ragged edges we are now treading.

(o) When we remember Isa. ch. 37 the awful havoc of a solitary angel responsively to the prophet's prayer, send down to Sennacherib's camp at midnight, when he slew 185,000 Assyrian soldiers; oh what will be the magnitudinous catastrophe wrought by a round milion in 45 years, Daniel's tribulation period 12;12), 1225 (12 ch 11 verse), giving 1290—45. You see (Dan. 12; 12) gives you 1335 days, and (v 11), 1290 das., elaving 45 yrs. the tribulation period, as you see in reading your Bible many revelations of the year day system, l. g. (ch. 9) He says it will be 70 weeks from the founding of the second temple by Ezra, Zerubbabel, and Nehemiah after the return out of Babylonian captivity in the fulfillment of Jer's prophecy, that the Chaldeans would carry them away and they would serve them 70 yrs.,

when they would send them back to rebuild    the
temple and the city: 70 weeks are 490 days.    His-
tory confirms the fact that it was just 490 years,
from the    founding of the second temple till    as
Daniel says, "Messiah would be cut off," i .e. Christ
crucified, which really transpired on that very day.

(p) When kings are shaken down, as we demon-
strated in the present wars, now desolating    the
Old World; heaping it with the slain and deluging
it in blood; the war not having originated with
the nations involved; but entirely with the    kings.
So it is really a magnitudinous trouble originating
from the fall of kings and    the    trepidation    of
others, lest they do fall.    So exceedingly formida-
ble of the implements of destruction;    tremendous
cannons, said to cost    a million dollars per gun,
made of the most costly material in all the world
and the machinery of the most valuable, expensive,
and efficient character; throwing great bomb shells
whose explosions tear cities to pieces and set them
on fire; immense gattling guns, sweeping down vast
multitudes like the scythe of the    steam    reaper,
taking fields with paradoxical expedition and mag-
nitude before them; the grandest and most unpre-
cented    inventions, of which the ages never dreamed, now brought into availibility, for the destruction of human life; the greatest powers of the earth,
combined and the profoundest    intellects    brought
into availibility in the machination of human destruc
tion;

(q)    The nations of the earth now throwing
wide open the door for all the inventions possible,
utterly regardless of cost; ready to pour out    a
princely fortune to anybody who can invent implements of homicide; ready to pay more to have people killed as rapidly as possible than any thing else;
awful to think, the highest premiums now paid for
wholesale destruction of human life, murder in the

sight of God who says "thou shalt not kill" Ex. 30 ch. I was a blooming youth, when the awful conferderate war broke out, deluging Dixie land with blood and draping Yankee mourning; parents weeping over their sons; widows and orphans wailing over fathers and husbands, cruelly shot down like the wild game on the mountain. I never went into the war and never in my life loaded a fire arm, nor learned to shoot. That glorious infantile conversion, the Lord gave me on my mother's lap, before she took off the baby clothes; felicitously saved me from ever going into the war. I would have rather laid down my own life, than to take the risk of killing some body else.

(r) The solution of the war problem is simple and easy; it is nothing but the device of Satan to fill up hell. If he had let us alone, Cain would have never killed Abel; thus manipulated by the devil to lead off the procession of murderers; destined to crimson the earth with blood and bleach it with the bones of the slain. When satan can get people into war, it is his grand camp meeting, both armies doing their best to kill each other, for no reason whatever. In the present war 1915 it is a notorious fact that these great nations, the largest on the globe had nothing at all to do with bringing it about and have nothing against each other; no reason why they should mutually run together and do their best like ferocious wild beasts to kill each other. It all came out of a little bit of a quarrel among the kings which they should have settled in their own private councils, without firing a gun. There is really nothing in it and never has been during the six thousand years of blood and death on the earth; actually killing 25 thousand millions of men, flooding the world with tears, blood, desolation, toil and sorrow and pouring into hell the revolving generations of humanity, for no

reason what ever except that the devil wants
hell populated and is determined to have it done at
every cost.

(s) Such is the awful armageddon now ominous-
ly preluded by the present bleeding Orient (Rev.
16:13), "I saw three unclean spirits, come out of
the mouth of the beast.  (Catholicism), the dragon
(Paganism) and the false prophet (Mohammedan) ;
the spirits of demons, working miracles and going
forth to gather the kings from the risng of the
sun to the great battle of God almighty, which is
the Armageddon.  While the present war is not the
Armageddon which will not take place till after the
rapture of the saints; because Daniel says every one
shall be delivered whose name is written in  the
book i. e. on the bride roll (12 ch.) as the rapture
of the saints has not yet taken place, we know that
the Armageddon has not set in; but the prophecies
all assure us that we are running into it, with an
alarming rapidity; oh what an inspiration to every
body to get saved through and through, robed and
ready for the glorious rapture of the saints! This
same scripture Rev. 16 ch. goes on "behold I come
as a thief! blessed is he that keepeth his garment,
 (i. e. his sanctified experience, a blood washed
robe) ; lest he walk naked, and they see his shame!"
Those who are really sanctified wholly, alone
are invested in this blood washed robe, made white
in the blood of Calvary's lamb.  Why does not every one take the warning and get ready, while they
can, to go up in the rapture of the saints, whose
prophetic panarama is actually moving in gorgeous
and thrilling admonition around every  luminous
Bible reader.

(t) Go on with this chapter and you'll run into
the last woe, proclaimed by the arch angel's trumpet and accompanied by the out  pouring of
the seventh and last plague on the earth  which

finishes up the wrath of God, against the wicked
nations and fallen churches  you  see  when this
angel pours out his bowl on the air,  lightnings,
thunders and earth quakes, immediately follow, in
all parts of the world; as the atmosphere envelopes
the whole earth and consequently the plague will
not be local as the trouble now in certain Oriental
countries; thus far leaving the great new  world
uninfected; which should inspire us all with grati-
tude to God and precipitated universal repentance
among sinners and consecration among all the Chris-
tians; waking up and walking in the light and avail-
ing themselves into the wonderful efficiency  of
precious blood, which cleanseth from all sin  and
gives victory to every soul (1 John 1:7) Oh how
we need gospel heralds running to the ends of the
slumbering millions, the momentous issues,  now
precipitated on them in the fulfilment of the thrilling latter day prophecies.

(n) When the destruction of Johnstown, Pa.,
by the flood was impending, the signs so strong
and obvious foreboding  the  bursting lake, that
the people all had opportunity to have escaped; yet
they did not take heed but went on with their mer-
chandise, their mechanisms and diversified employ-
ments; dispite all the obvious and impending warning not only did many people go through the city
warning them to escape for their lives; but a man
on a fleet horse rode through it shouting aloud, the
lake is breaking, the lake is bursting, all fly to the
mountains! of course some took heed and saved
their lives meanwhile the multitude staid  with
their stuff, till it was too late and perished in the
sweeping deluge; flooding the city twenty to  a
hundred feet deep and sweeping the multitudes
into eternity.

(u)  The great Orient wars, involving Britain,
the greatest power on the earth, Russia next, then

Germany, France and Turkey, the five greatest nations in the old world as well as a number lesser
powers; already involved in this terrible conflict,
the monitory prelude of the great tribulation; destined soon to wrap the whole world in deadly conflict; but, one real security and that is the glorious
rapture of the saints. Therefore we cannot afford
to take any risk on this momentous issue. Oh
how the whole world now needs the good old plain
straight gospel, the only fortification against the
myriads of satanic delusions; multitudious coun-
terfeits hatched in hell. You can easily discrim-
inate the trues from the false if you will note the
fact, that Christ alone can save us all; the true
preacher of the gospel, all standing in the im-
mediate succession of John the Baptist who cried
aloud behold the Lamb of God, that taketh away
the sin of the world. Here we see sin in the
singular number. Our sins are always in the plural
as they are absolutely innumerable in thought,
word and deed; being the millions of poisonous ap-
ples produced by the deadly upas tree; whereas the
sin of the world, is the tree itself. Get rid of that
and you never have any more of the obnoxious
hell produced fruits; condemnatory and destructive
world without end. In regeneration, not only is
all you're own condemnatory sins swept away; by
the mighty besom of justifying grace, and a new
heart and a new spirit given, transforming you
into a ew creature; yet the old ma of sin has
only been conquered and bound and you still have
him on hand, and he will lead you to commit more
sins and plunge you deep into former condemnation;
precipitating you into a backsliding hell; whereas you must move unhesitatingly and seek the cru-
cifition of the sin personality, which Jesus
gives you whe He baptizes you with the Holy
Ghost and fire (Rom. 6:1, 6;) thus crucifying the

old man of sin, i. e. digging out the upas tree by the
roots and burning it up root and branch, with the
fires of the Holy Ghost, i. e having crucified the old
man of sin as you see his body is destroyed an
that body, buried not into water, as false prophets
deceive you; but into the death of Christ, which
is the atonement he made for all sin; in order to
utterly take away the sin of the world and give
you a clean heart, which is none other than the
blood washed robe, worn by all the saints, consti-
tuting the bridehood, for whom the Lord is coming,
to take them up to the marriage supper of the
lamb; before the great Armageddon moves out in
full blast to eliminate out of the world all of the
unsaveable and incorrigibles; multiplied millions of
whom, have already crossed the dead line,
grieved away the Holy Spirit and settled the mat-
ter, beyond defalcation, that they will not let God
save them. Therefore divine mercy says cut them
down before they commit more sins; thus piling up
wrath against the day of wrath and the righteous
judgments of the sin avenging God.

(w) While the true preacher, sent of God, in
a secession of John Baptist, hides behind the cross
and cries "Behold the Lamb of God, which taketh
away the sin of the world," i. e. takes out of you
and as God says cast it into the sea of forgetful-
ness; thus saving you from wrath.  . .

x) Thus you always differentiate God's prophets from Satan's by the simple fact that they
hide behind the cross and cry "Behold the Lamb
of God that taketh away the sin of the world"
(John 1: 29.) In the heroic succession of John
the Baptist the honored introducer of Christ and the
precursor of the Gospel dispensation; whereas
Satan's preachers always take you into custody,
proselyte you into their sect or denomination and
send you to the water-god, the eucharist or some

other ecclesiastical divinity; e. g. great Catholicism with his 450 millions of members and 2 million preachers; the priests themselves claiming the power to take away sins, meanwhile themselves the greatest sinners you can find. In this country Campbellites and Mormon prophets, are on the very same line, giving you the water-god, weak as water, a dumb helpless idol, like the wooden and stone gods of great Pagandom. Therefore luminous people with an open Bible are left without excuse. No wonder I am running to the ends of the earth and doing my best to get all Holiness people who have the experience, supernaturally born (John 3:7) and sanctified wholly (Heb. 12:14), to go and preach this wonderful gospel to the 1,700 millions, now thronging this Bible world; amid universal verifications of our Savior's lugubrious proclamation

> "Broad is the road that leads to death
> And thousands walk together there,
> While wisdom shows a narrow path
> With here and there a traveller."

Showing up the multitude on their way to hell while the saved are few; a similar preponderance of the Satanic ministry over the Lord's faithful prophets who cry aloud and spare not; ready for decapitation rather than compromise.

---

## Chapter III.

## FALL OF SATAN AND ALL THE KINGS

You see this thrillingly portrayed (Rev. ch. 19) all the kings on the fied and fighting with all their might to hold their kingdoms viz. the Lord Jesus

Christ in the capacity of a mounted warrior, riding forth conquering and to conquer. You see them all go down in bood; thus forfeiting their thrones scepters and crowns after a reign of 6000 years never to regain them. In this grand panorama, you see the ubiquity of the Armageddon revealed and confirmed in the proclamation of the Angel standing on the sun and vociferating to all the carniverous beasts and birds in the whole world a royal invitation to the greatest banquet ever enjoyed in the roll of the ages; thus extending the table around the world, groaning under the fallen kings, queens, princes, potentates and the multitudes of their servants in every land and clime; thus sweeping away the popular apprehension of a local Armageddon; as this angel herald stands on the sun, it will only take 24 hours for the proclamation to reach every carniverous beast and bird in all the earth; thus rendezvousing to the grand banquet to feast on the flesh of all the people in the world ,who will not let God save them; thus verifying the utility of the great Armageddon, i. e. to eliminate out of the world al the unsavables and incorrigibles, who will not do for the glorious oncoming millenial reign, when "righteousness peace and joy (Rom. 14; 17) will fill the whole earth and He shall have dominion o'er river sea and shore; far as the eagles pinion or doves light wing can soar; when the glowing anticipations, sung by the gospel heralds through the long rolling ages, will be signally, jubilantly and triumphantly verified;

"From Greenland's icy mountain;
From India's coral strand;
Where Afric's sunny fountain
Rolls down the golden sand;
From many an ancient river;
From many a palmy plain,

They call us to deliver
Their land from error's chain!

Shall we whose souls are lighted
With wisdom from on high?
Shal we to men benighted,
The lamb of life deny?
Waft, wafe ye winds His story
And you you waters roll;
Till like a sea of glory
It spreads from pole to pole!

Till o'er our ransomed nature,
The Lamb for sinner's slain;
Redeemer, King, Creator,
In bliss returns to reign."

In this fall of all the kings from their thrones, remember (Rev. ch 18) that Babylon falls to rise no more i. e. Satan's religions are actually swept from the face of the earth; leaving nothing but straight sky blue regeneration and sun burst sanctification, to fill the whole world with the glory of God; Satan's long reign of 6000 years, accompanied by floods and oceans of idolatry in conceivable ramification worshipping priests and potentates, living and dead; church rites, ordinances, ceremonies, good works and everything machinated in the bottomless pit and used to sidetrack the people, from the kings highway of holiness unto the Lord Isa 35 ch.

(y) Rev. ch. 19 you see all the kings fall from their thrones, never to regain them; pope and Mohammed, Satans right and left bowers both arrested alive and cast into the lake of fire and brimstone, far away in outer darkness a 1000 years before the devil gets there; Babylon having hopelessly fallen and God's merciful proclamation ringing in

seraphic melodies, cordially inviting all who will let
God save them, to come out, get saved and live forever. You see also the fall of Satan himself and
his imprisonment in hell. The oncoming millenial
reign; his myrmidons, all having been cast out;
thus sweeping away every obstruction to the glory
of the Lord, destined to cover the whole earth as the
waters cover the sea. Now we see (ch 20) the
angel, (Michael I trow) come down from heaven,
having in his hand the key to the bottomless pit;
lay hold on the dragon that old serpent who is the
devil and Satan, bind him fast, cast him into the
pandemonium there to be a lugubrious prisoner
while the millenial centuries come and go. We see
Rev. 9; 1 Satan's fall from heaven, when he was
cast out and that he has the key of hell and opens
it, when the Mohammedan armies symbolized by
voracious locusts pour out and spread destruction
over the whole world; confirmatory of the conclusion that as the king of hell he has had the
key al these 6000 years; yet you see in this scripture, that the police angel has it and uses it against
him; opening the door, casting him in and locking
him up a hopeless prisoner, without a chance for
a trial or anything else and doomed to while away
a thousand years; thus confirming the conclusion,
that in the Armageddon wars, the trend will
eventually turn terrifically against him, so he will
lose ground; suffering crushing defeats, despite all
his efforts to utilize his armies demoniacal and human; Etygian and terrestrial; suffering an actual
chain of catastrophes, so breaking his power, that
he is utterly unable to hold it any longer; when
signal and hopeless defeat, settles down like a
nightmare on the innumerable armies encircling the
world with the Armageddon phalanx; getting more
and more impetuous in its downward rush, ultimat-
ing in signal and hopeless defeat; all the Kings,

queens, princes, and potentates going down in the
world ecircling massacre and turned over to all the
voracious, carniverous beasts and birds to come and
enjoy the royal banquet of the ages, commemorat-
ing Satan's final and hopeless defeat, when with
mournful wails he  and  all his myrmidons retreat
from the fields.  When Gen. Lee surrendered to
Grant in 1865, I was Pres. of a  college  in  In-
diana and in  the  suburbs coming home, when suddenly the most impetuous bell ringing I ever heard
began in the college and spread throughout  the
town, till everything that could make a noise was in
a clatter.  I was young and a fleet runner and heed-
ing the alarm sped with all my might.  By the time
I reached the streets I found them thronged with
men, women and children from the hoary head to
the cradle toddler; everybody in their work habit
as they happened to be; women with their hands in
dough, dishereled hair,  and  everyone  something
to make a noise; meanwhile shouting aloud; cannons
roading not only in that town but others far  and
near we heard on all sides; a lightning courier having dispatched the neews, Lees surrendered to Grant
and  the  long  bloody  was  at  an  end.

(z) When Cornwallis at Yorktown surrendered to
Washington, every British soldier laid down his
gun and fired it no more; so soon as the tardy tid-
ings around the world.

"The hero chieftain laying down his pen,
Closes his eyes in Washington at ten;
The lightning courier leaps along the line
And tells the St. Louis tale at nine!
Halting a thousand miles whence he departed,
And getting there an hour before he started."

These paradoxical news facilities, thus enabled
great Dixie Land to receive, as well as Yankeedom

the thrilling news in a few fleeting moments . The
result was every Confederate soldier laid down his
gun and fired it no more; proceeding at once to
hunt up his plow and proceed to plant his cotton
as in the days of yore, when he bossed the obse-
quious darkies to plow and hoe, gather the crops,
and clothe the world in cotton. In a similar man-
ner when the Apocalyptic Angel shall come down,
arrest the devil and take him out of the world;
every myrmidon will skeedadde with all possible expedition; the demoniacal armies glad of a chance
to retreat before the triumphant host of Prince Im-
manuel, the conqueror of Mt. Calvary, against
whom they have been arrayed these memorable
6000 years; all the time cheered by their triumphant king Diabolus on the throne of the world, with
all the kings and their mighty armies, bringing vas-
sals at his feet; the carnal millions of earth
all obsequions to their satanic majesty; triumphant from the rising of the sun to the going down
of the same, girdling the world with their shouts
of victory; but now they are all gone; the kings,
queens, satraps and satanic subordinates of every
and nation, swept away; their great king Diabolus himself a pitiful prisoner, committed to the
dungeon a thousand years. Consequently, the myrmidons who have had their barracks in the air six
thousand years are glad of a chance to retreat away
and take their places in the gloomy regions of the
pandimonium where they have countless millions
of company, all on their side and homeogenions
with them. While the stygian milions are retreat-
ing from this world, I expect to do some big shouting. That will be a wonderful epoch in the his-
tory of saints and anges; the latter all having been
thrillingly interested in the creation of this world
and we know not to what extent, honored with the
participation in that stupendous work; so that when

God had finished it, shining in his edenic splendor,. beauty and glory, they all shouted for joy; thus responsively to the anthem of the morning stars which sang together, and all the sons of God shouted for joy  When the news of Eden's fall reached Heaven, it is said that all the angels  hung their golden harps on weeping willows and broke out in lugubrious wails bemoaning the awful catastrophe, till the son of God walking out on the celestial battlements proclaimed to them his espousal of the lost cause.  Then they knew that victory was at hand. Consequently taking down their harps they tuned them to more brilliant melodies augmented by· the transporting anthems of redeeming  grace  and dying love; thus giving a new inspiration to the jubilant celestial and audiences, who from that day till this have with renewed interest, thronged this world serving as our guardian angels.  "The angel of the Lord encampeth round about them that fear Him and delivereth them."  Oh blessed consolation, the loving sympathetic guardian angels!

....          FINIS          ....

# Apostolic Holiness Sunday School Literature

**APOSTOLIC BIBLE TEACHER**
A Monthly Journal for Sunday School
Teachers

**THE ADVANCED QUARTERLY**
Prepared for the Advanced Sunday School
Classes

**YOUNG PEOPLE'S QUARTERLY**
For Intermediate Sunday School Classes

**THE CHILDREN'S PAPER**
Especially prepared for Primary Classes
Ably edited from a full salvation stand-
point. Will raise the spiritual life
of any Sunday School

**SECRETARY'S COMPLETE RECORD**
For the Secretary a whole year

**TEACHER'S CLASS BOOK**
For the Teacher a whole year

Samples sent free on application

Published by the
APOSTOLIC MESSENGER OFFICE
GREENSBORO, N. C.